the curse of immortality

Mei Sayre

BookLeaf Publishing

India | USA | UK

the curse of immortality © 2024 Mei Sayre

All rights reserved.

No part of this publication may be reproduced, stored in a retrieval system, or transmitted, in any form or by any means, electronic, mechanical, photocopying, recording or otherwise, without the prior written permission of the presenters.

Mei Sayre asserts the moral right to be identified as the author of this work.

Presentation by *BookLeaf Publishing*

Web: www.bookleafpub.com

E-mail: info@bookleafpub.com

ISBN: 9789363317970

First edition 2024

To my beloved readers,

I offer you my soul, laid bare upon the page,

as proof of immortality.

destrudo

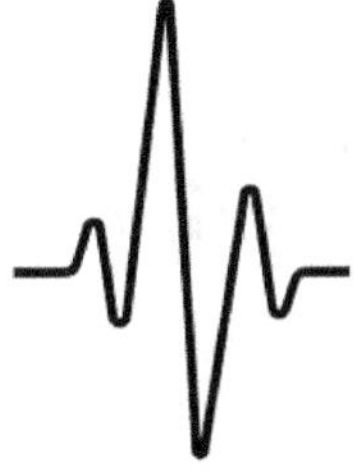

I spent my best three years racing
on a hamster wheel and trying not to lose.
New York was meant to be a new beginning but
it wasn't. Unless you count losing everything,
downing a bottle of pills and waking up dead
two days later in the same room.
It doesn't make a difference. I was just
tired for some weeks,
my heart was always pounding, and
heat made me feel weak, which was worse
since it was summer. Go on like
nothing happened. Keep going.

I gaze at the skyline across the East River,
beautiful and haunting,
no matter how many times I pass
the first light that chases away the likes of us,
when I find myself alive. Maybe I'm
upside down again, and in my head so
nobody hears me scream in a void where

existence terrifies me. But not nearly as much as these seven years of stagnation that strike down paths I can't reach. I used to write stories about falling in love and now I can't love anything. You're just a bunch of words on a page and the letters don't make any sense.

twenty-one days

I'm still in love
with the thought of you
like a snapshot in my mind
like a monument standing brave that
never weathered with time

I fell in love with the start of things
promises just outside my reach
I always thought to hold them dear
since you left them in my care

You laid your head upon my chest
burrowed deep within my heart
made a home of me, and
now I feel you every time I draw a breath

You left me wandering, and

wildly in love
with the memories of us
rise up like ghosts under the candles lit to
hold vigil with me because you
abandoned me at last

If I could turn back time
I would make you say goodbye because
my youth is better spent
alone with me than
so alone with you

When we parted for the final time
I died within myself, tonight
I vow to
die again for you

And since it can't be that I miss you
I must be in love
with the thought of you.

lux and luminosity

borne under the shadow for the folly of another
for mistakes were ever made, both selfish and
in vain, every day she begged for mercy
but mercy never came
unwillingly she caved and she fell into tomorrow

she was enamored with her heroes
and falling to his knees, he presented her
with gifts filled up with splendor, grief and
honesty, all wrapped up in ribbons luxe
tendrils of living luminosity

as she toiled and labored to find her place
in bygone days he slipped away
a hero's promise to the god's forsaken left her
awaiting his return
for all of time

and this treasure that he gave her,
a gilded vessel filled with dreams that
tempted to fly open with a flutter of her lips
a kiss, perhaps, carrying whisperings of
love, about the first we ever shared and the
mysteries of us

young Pandora was a fool, as she came
to understand
but it's part of growing up

the unknown's a brutal curse,
she's still learning to
let go, because all the evils in the world
flew out and took over her mind
only the remainder, a drop of hope found
tangled in the threads
she wears it as a necklace and
it keeps her moving on

summer solstice

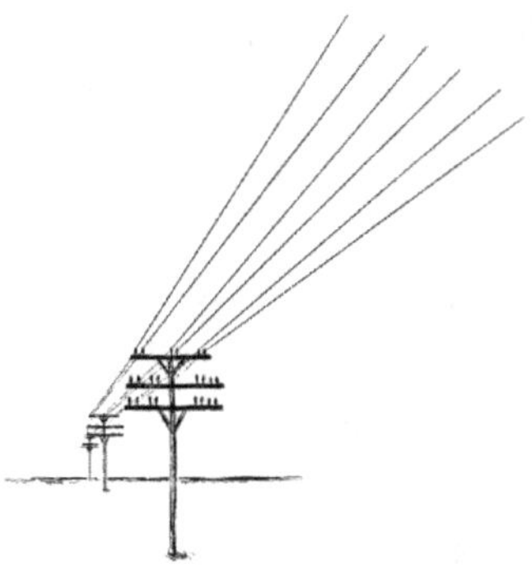

impulse runaway
power lines run by in blur
the train tracks set direction

straight ahead with purpose
and to the bitter end
until all the passengers are leaving

but there's no destination for me yet
perpetually adrift and aimless
chasing what I may never reach

count the time to the last station
ride until there's nowhere left to go
wander empty roads as I try to find home

tossed out, let go, alone and otherworldly

unaccepted and out of luck
hit that dead end running

don't say it gets better someday
I can't see that for myself
so wait for me in another life

we head deeper into the city,
where its dust covers the sunrise
still lights up the sky

and I pray to anyone out there,
through my fears
wear me down, cloud my hopes

still shine through, courage
leads me out to seek someplace
I'll be invited, always

until the door finally opens and
our eyes meet, through my tears
we embrace once again.

my forever and always
that I turned upside down
but here and now,

you flip that, and
what's always been wrong,

you make right.

so please
don't tell me I'm dreaming
because this is all what's meant to be

colors too bright to see
clarity hurts my eyes
it's so surreal to me

thinking too much
trying too hard
cry until it hurts

with nothing left to prove
so just burn a hole in me
and look right through.

we fall like night at dusk
drift off in peace
as Venus rises slowly

at the end of summer solstice
her prayers lift us up
and shower us in the afterglow.

the silence

sit next to me
can we talk about the pressure
yes, that one, the one you still claim
you don't know about

that which compresses the mind
until it becomes pure, faraway, lost
like the corners of the universe, ever in flux
from the beginning of time
and when was that, for you?

that which tightens your vocal cords
feel like knots, don't make a sound
turn your fingers into ice,
you can't stretch them out
flash freeze everything that you can see,

a life in eternal permafrost

you wonder if it's for the best
promise there's no choice but to accept
you believe such reality, and so it goes
and let the silence set you free

cover all the mirrors in the room
no reflections, cast no shadows
in a painless snow-white landscape
no need to search for colors or contrast
in the self-inflicted solitude

but you still love what you love
so die, and die again, without reprieve
you only go forward because there is no back

there's nothing behind you
so don't turn around

here, now
for a moment, focus
look, and you find yourself
a single point compressed
within all four dimensions

yet you're expanding like the universe

drugs

it gets
weary
to me
the loss
the religion
the rise and the fall
the rinse and repeat
and the never enough
the sanity you question
when it's been enough days
and you start to doubt yourself
so you get lost in the mistakes you've made
and regret and hatred that spiral down into hell

but the dawn
and the trust
and the peace
and the warmth
that connects you to
yourself and someone else
until it creates bonds
that can't be broken,
with any space or time
cuts so deep, pierces into you
settles in and stays, because
it's found where it's meant to be

so watch as the lights glow more
than you've ever seen them glow before
and feel the air against your skin
making you alive for the first time in your life
so talk to me because I've never felt
the words you say so deeply as I do now
and I've never understood anything as much
as I understand you right now

if you want
to see truth
then find me
at the horizon
past the terminus
I stand at every day
and the memories locked away
and the hope when there was none
in a place long lost in my history

revived only by an elixir
that makes every place on earth
somewhere I feel safe,
because I fear myself the most,
and I never escape me
so I craft a bottle of new halcyon days
Elysian Fields upon these streets
to roam before my time is up

sends all these years
of buried pain away
like fine breeze upon dandelion seeds
carrying them up into blue skies
to set me free

somnia

the days were
comfortably numb

one morning I arose to find myself
bathed in glistening rosewater and flower petals
in a paradise of crystalline fountains

waking up dazed because I had been in repose
for about seven years and at the end
I realized something
was wrong

the owner of this house is missing

borrowed years, on borrowed strength
filthy lies, what a magnificent fight

The owner of this house has gone missing

where is she?
She's not here anymore

left without a note or anything
maybe on a vacation
seems like she was tired, been working too hard,
every day, nonstop, to keep this thing afloat

so she left me in charge

and look at the mess I've made,
five months in and the place is a mess
laundry piled up, dirty dishes in the sink
dozens of unopened letters, bursting with bills

they ask how she's doing
when she'll be back

I can reach out for you
I mean, she's just a step away for me
She'll come back to us, I'm sure
She always does, she's so reliable

I'm sure you all know that
it's what everyone says
She's not like me at all

what do you need?
can I help you, since you're here?

can I do the same?

I can do the same, can't I?

a battle to save the world

this fight isn't worth it
like they promised it would be

we grew up, sprouted wings
caught the last bus of the evening
said goodbye to our hometowns
with no idea where we were headed

but I heard this was the road to paradise.
now we're burned out and blacked out
and we don't remember how we got here
all we know is that we've come too far to go

feels like it was all just talk,
of the battered and brilliant
blind faith we'd make it better
after burdens and burials got us playing the hero

all that we open up about in privacy
whispers behind rotating doors
you show up outside at 2 AM, no warning
turn off the lights and fall into my bed

your arms lock around me, anchor me to you
kisses so deep they feel like you're
asking me to save you.

so I say I will, if you save me

we trade bodies, trade souls, trade each other,
betray ourselves
dip into debts we know we can't afford
and pray these secrets die with us

late night trips with your hands in my hair
and my thighs on your hips
beg me for release,
pent up fears, grief, anger, tears

always told to be brave, stay strong, do better
but we're exhausted and drained
from long hours we battle
blurred eyes, lost fights, chasing futile victory

because we gave up our youth for this
and it's best not to think about it
but damn, it hurts to remember
the way things were, and could have been

so we lie together, like lovers
listen to the air and words that don't mean much
we talk dreams, big dreams
about the things that mattered

how you run on pure ambition,

eyes on that bright finish line up ahead as for
me, I don't have much to live for
but I want to change the world

and then you tell me that I'm special
hell, I wish I were
yours.

and there I go, lying to myself,
delusions of intimacy
knowing your time for me is measured
in seconds and stressors and scales

tangled up in the sheets
with my face against your chest
it's too hot, too close, it's hard to breathe
I pull away for air but you pull me back

you say, "stay, it feels good"

so I stay and let you burn me.
and we fall asleep together in my bed
for a blissful few hours,
and barely after sunrise you're awake

"stay."

if only I could tell you that
I need you right now,

but we aren't here for things like that
so I don't say anything

it might not be the life I asked for
but this is all I have for now
to escape within, I find myself
caught beneath the undercurrent

of the nights we spend to protect
the shreds of our cadavers
key in variations of codes we
won't ever bother to remember

racing past and stepping over,
all that we crush beneath our feet
until we're left defenseless.
I saw it last August, one afternoon

you said you "had to get away from it all,"
looking up at me with your head in my lap,
I caress your face and see you smile
giving me your vulnerability.

all of this, I know it never mattered
and you think you're so invincible but
you came to me
when you burned out, broke down

it's morning,

time to go

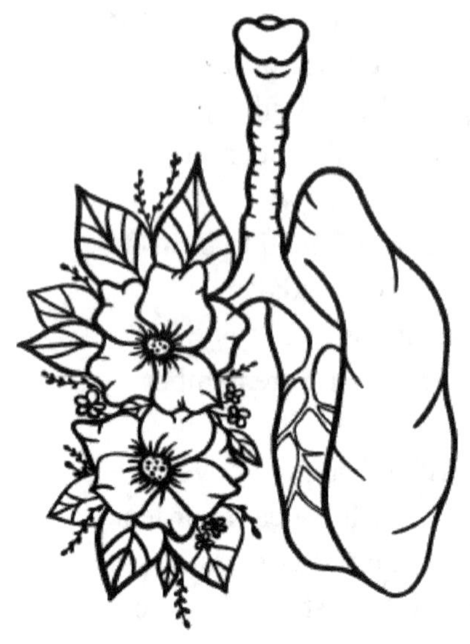

the end of immortality

meet me by the spirited stream, astir with songs
past the back of beyond
this land is where the beginning meets the end

a silver snake rears her head at me
before she twists around and sinks
fangs into her tail
death, rebirth, the cycle of life
ends here with me

I've watched the world burn before my eyes
so much it's etched into my soul
I spread the ashes across the ocean
from which we may rise once more

aquamarine, foam of the sea
golden wings across a sunless sky
we give meaning for things we don't know
a firefly, three shooting stars, so promise me

you'll catch me when I fall
down from the heavens so
your eyes are the first thing I'll ever see
and remind me again of my responsibility

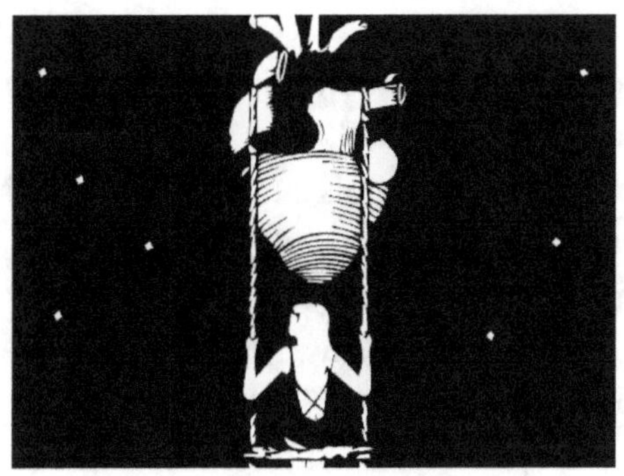

castle of air

It felt so easy and happened so quickly, they say
I must have been insane
to throw my life away but I don't think it's all
that unsound, for me to
so easily
give up on the dream I'd been chasing
for the better part of a decade, and right before I
had it in my hands

and that's because I knew this would happen, as
far back as I remember.
So long that I was slowly preparing for my
downfall since childhood, so long that I feel
amazed it
took almost thirty years for this character I built
to finally
break.

I used to think I wouldn't live past eighteen,
become anything at all, least of which
a doctor, the type who's supposed to save lives
and take care of sick people
when I couldn't save myself and felt just as
sick as the patients I saw. Maybe that was
meant to be
irony, and part of the allure of it all,
but I am relieved that I won't need to pretend to
look halfway sane in a white coat ever again.

It happened in a split second, with me dreaming
and wide awake at the same time
a cataclysmic decision is made, with just a bit of
collateral damage. Then it was over.
Years of efforts vanish the way I once fantasized
about, feared, and coveted,
and my shackles have been broken at last.

Ask me if I care.
At least I'll never have to wake up at 5 AM
every day again
to the sound of that vile alarm.

In my new life I can sleep and wake up
whenever I want.
No one will talk bad about me or
hurt me, in any way at all.

I'll make another world and make it last forever,
tell me I'm mistaken
and I'll tell you that you're wrong.
I know this for certain because
somehow I always manage to get
what I want in life,
even until the breaking point, and even after, I
had it my way.

I confess that I've wanted to give up, fall apart,
lose my mind
ever since I was young but I could never commit
to it because
what is imperfection? No idea, but it sounds
peaceful.

We are taught to be strong and so
when I start I never stop. Sunk cost fallacy had
me submerged
down deeper with every step
of the way and until I learned that brute force
works until it doesn't.

Because all along I thought I was
being strong but
I was foolish.

Now I let go of the perfect life I
sacrificed myself for

which was so, so limited I didn't see the
sky for years because I thought
I wasn't allowed
to look up.

I'd just about gone insane
a few hundred times already
but my mind always clung on like a signal that I
was meant for
something far greater.
But that was wrong and the truth is that
the greatness is at the bottom and from there
it reveals itself and opens
a path skyward.

screaming

let me tell you about the hatred and anger
and the things I won't forgive
because if it's so wrong to destroy myself then
I'm better off destroying you all

in this world we talk so much about
the lesser of two evils, to pick your poison
and the like of making such facile decisions
so I picked up a few too many poisons

enough to last a lifetime for me and
twelve more suffering souls
but there are some I haven't tasted
and I'd be glad to test them all at once
if it changes anything, because

it sure looks like society's still not satisfied

they say, if you find your true self then you'll
know what you really want to be
but I've known myself all along
if you truly insist, I'll speak it

keep in mind that ever since the first time,
I've tried not to know
because I couldn't bear to, and when I could
I decided not to because I was going to
be better than that

but if I've run out of options, as I very much
seem to have
been pushed into a corner yet again
then I won't avert my eyes any longer for sake
of unreciprocated decency, because

I'm not what you think I am.

there's a cage in a place that I call home where
no one ever goes because anyone who does
would die

I pretend it's not there but I've been there before
and I'll never forget the smell of chains
there was a child screaming at the top of her
lungs and when I saw what she looked like

I felt too sick to stay but I couldn't
tear my eyes away or
tear my eyes out

sometimes I hear it still
even though I'm outside
sometimes it gets loud, so loud it
drowns out all my thoughts

I don't know where it comes from but I think it's
everywhere
I'm the only one who knows her but she's not
inside my head
she never says an actual word, so I can't
tell why she's there

what I do know is that I, too, would scream
if I were her

flashbacks like a soundscape

last year was a nightmare
woke up in a new room
sheets soaked in cold sweat
still trapped in a dream world
forever home in this prison

blurred out in a bad trip
flashbacks like a soundscape
race fast through the green light
spray paint all the skies red
screams ring loud in my ears

all the people are monsters
every word is a threat
the air smells like fumes
but I can't find the fire

they're all out to get me
I'd run but I'm tied down
hide with no sanctuary
no, they won't take us alive
I'll fight to the death

just push it all back down
suppress all the hatred
paranoia is daylight

hold my head underwater
and don't let me breathe

say we'll never be safe here
so shut the door tight behind you
keep your heart closed on lockdown
stay behind, build up high walls
and don't let them pass through

I won't let them hurt you
if anyone peeks through
they'll be sure to break you
ice cold but it's all truth
dead weight but it saves you

what I would give now
to trust like I used to

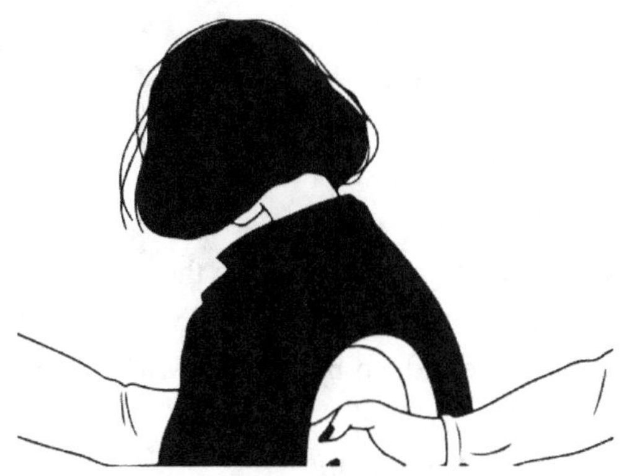

your goodbye

I wore my heart on my sleeve
of the jacket I left in your car that crashed
off the Brooklyn Bridge last week

resuscitate me, over and over
for all of my life

I beg them to stop but no sound can escape
paralytics keep me bound even as
the anesthesia runs low, far too soon

I write poetry in my mind as I wait
for the signal to scream
while strangers and lovers
and demons and gods fight to

keep me alive, against
my best efforts
pull me back underwater

now I'm standing naked before the last jury and
I have no defense for myself and what I've done
I'm here to be judged but I'm unworthy at best

let this world trample me
a doll made of paper and glass

shred me up with the current

thank you for staying with me
until the end.

until the stars burn out

You are my fire.
You are the sun and the dawn
as it explodes in the morning sky.

You are a portal to another realm,
an alternate dimension I neither see nor feel
but I will gladly lose myself to you.
Let me remain there for all eternity,
never to return.
Let me stay, grow old, and die with you.

I may never come to find
what is real or what is right.
Now that all the lines are blurred, let's
burn them all away, and break free
of these constraints that tether us-

And to think, it started off as nothing
you make it out to be so easy.
Letter by letter, slow dripping into me like
an intravenous line,
the light on the screen as I'm buried
under covers, are we really here together?

Alone in this room, falling in a haze.
Sleep and wake interconnect until
everything is you. Do you know how it
feels when
everything is you?

How could I ever tell you?
I could never,
but who was I fooling anyway?
Who would have believed me
if I told them it felt real?
But it isn't real, is it?
Our love, it's so one-sided.

I am your fire.
I will love you until the stars burn out.

I will love you even after.

colors

they tell me I'm a walking time-bomb
and it's too late to defuse
just stay away, it's for the best
and when I find myself alone
there's a power surge, I can't deny
I feel the remaining seconds
melting through my skin

pastel sky blue
chains made of clouds
wrapped around my left wrist
five hundred miles long and pulling me north
that had gently guided me for many
months lost at sea, so hold fast
until it began to drag me so hard it nearly
shattered my bones

I screamed to let go and clouds turned into rain
since then the chain has worn and decayed
and I can't bear to gaze at Polaris again

everything you were to me is
cold as the hail that
hits my window
while my clock and I consort

red like roses, edge of flame, the glow of rubies,
and wine-stained dresses, a live wire
buried in my right arm that runs through
my bloodstream
before it bursts from my skin and dashes
four million feet and finds home
as a permanent fixture in
the ghost town of your memories
and it haunts me

there's a vacuum that pulls all the air
out this room and I haven't breathed
ever since

that night I remembered I was free
tick, tock
the choice was mine
red or blue?

and I laughed because no one was coming to
save me
before I exploded
a sickening heap of existential dread

so I tore the red out of me that
burrowed deep into my heart and
cut the blue that had always
showed me the way home
and the colors of my insides
were beautiful
all over the bathroom floor
and the mirrors and ceiling

as if no one had ever been there

juliet

I'll be the cosmos
that light up your sky

tonight you'll fall asleep
as I fill up your soul

wrapped up in secrets
short of a miracle
just so you know
how close I dance with death

so speak to me
with words that I don't hear

and I don't know
if I'll ever let you see

these terrifying truths
that are eating me alive

spill all these secrets
like syrup, melted and sweet
kisses from my mouth
slide over your tongue, tied
so you promise me
that you'll never tell a soul
take me
so I can tangle you in vines
spill your blood with thorns
and twist your head with lies
the fucking insincerity
of reality and I

so I'll tell you how
it breaks my heart
to rise from the abyss
and walk this earth
wearing the mask of an angel
I don't deserve, but

I still want to be your miracle
so let me disappear
spare you, before you find
I'm not how you envision me

so goodnight, in whispers

as the sky watches over you
glimmering in silence
for all eternity

romeo

these nights become longer
without you in my arms, reach over to hold you,
touch you, protect you
I want you dozing off, next to me in my bed
appearing in my mind, my every fantasy
you're my muse
I want to share your breath, life into
my emptiness

it's so simple but it hurts,
I can't bear to dream of you

I want you more than I can phrase,
I want to say more
than there are words to describe
the many ways I need you
and these words aren't mine to say,

while you're in my clothes
you're on my mind
the feel of your body is all over my skin
the taste of you is still on my lips
it's in my reach, it's in my reach
you're the only thing that fills my mind
when I'm half asleep, still waking up
delirious, fever dreams

I'm out of my mind
because I need you here
it's getting cold and I'm missing out
lock me up in this room, and hold me close
I want to be alone with you,
for a while,
let's block out the world
I'd do that for you if you'd give me a chance

cross my heart and hope to die.

this is how we fall in love

a confession to make
call it a terrible mistake
I can't stop thinking of you
and it's worse every day

this is a story about falling in love
and letting go when I realized
it wasn't enough

I've told it before but I'll tell it again

how we met in the springtime,
both lost to the world
young and confused, still with
nothing to lose

we collide like a storm, passion and fury
lightning and thunder have nothing on us
time passes by but it's never too much
you're my warmth through the icy rain

I spent forever hoping someone would save me

you're all of my life
and all of the next one
I broke down in the madness

of summer's reverie
as I dance on the ledge
caught by your silhouette

fall apart, rise again
stronger now 'til the end
couldn't find my way through
but I'm blessed to see you visit me
in my dreams, fall in love

wake up holding treasures
of our shared memories

wings

the hardest part is letting
go of the life we shared
which is now everything to me
looking back
around, ahead and even
all the places I fail to see

If I were a puppet master pulling
all the strings in this world
I would use it to keep you safe
build an isolation chamber of our own
that no one else could enter
from which we need not ever leave

so that I could forever shelter you because
I wish I had made you stay
If I had wings, I would take you far away
and invent a new life where everything is right
fly you to a planet that I'd discover just for you
where the sky glows kaleidoscopic
unless the stars are out
and flowers bloom in snow the way you do
the seasons summon cloudbursts
that melt into rising tides
because you love standing in the rain

If I could make every word I write
blossom to existence before our eyes
with the ink from this pen sinking slow
into every sheet
as they pile up beside me
then even if all my remaining years were
spent laboring at this desk
I'd craft an entire universe for you
the fabric of your dreams with my
lifeblood from my fingertips
to bring you to the fantasies you crave

I, alone, would write forever for you

liquid gold and literature

you're liquid gold and literature
poured over me unfiltered
overflow me with lyrics, rhyme, and lore
we're so lovely, sad, and sinful

you turn hellfire that tears through
every page of me, this and that and more
now hold still if you feel the rhythm
of my weary heart, it trembles

I'm done, over, and ruined
from times temptation led me astray
it's woven red across my skin
in threads of detached punishment

leave me anchored by the empty shore
cherish me with your glow
may our silence someday come to pass
I'll be here, unaltered truth and yours

www.ingramcontent.com/pod-product-compliance
Lightning Source LLC
LaVergne TN
LVHW021255200726
843509LV00012B/1677